W9-CLM-666

ANIMALS OF THE FOREST

Gray Wolves

by Al Albertson

BLASTOFF!
2
READERS

BELLWETHER MEDIA · MINNEAPOLIS, MN

Note to Librarians, Teachers, and Parents:

Blastoff! Readers are carefully developed by literacy experts and combine standards-based content with developmentally appropriate text.

Level 1 provides the most support through repetition of high-frequency words, light text, predictable sentence patterns, and strong visual support.

Level 2 offers early readers a bit more challenge through varied simple sentences, increased text load, and less repetition of high-frequency words.

Level 3 advances early-fluent readers toward fluency through increased text and concept load, less reliance on visuals, longer sentences, and more literary language.

Level 4 builds reading stamina by providing more text per page, increased use of punctuation, greater variation in sentence patterns, and increasingly challenging vocabulary.

Level 5 encourages children to move from "learning to read" to "reading to learn" by providing even more text, varied writing styles, and less familiar topics.

Whichever book is right for your reader, Blastoff! Readers are the perfect books to build confidence and encourage a love of reading that will last a lifetime!

This edition first published in 2020 by Bellwether Media, Inc.

No part of this publication may be reproduced in whole or in part without written permission of the publisher. For information regarding permission, write to Bellwether Media, Inc., Attention: Permissions Department, 6012 Blue Circle Drive, Minnetonka, MN 55343.

Library of Congress Cataloging-in-Publication Data

Names: Albertson, Al, author.
Title: Gray Wolves / by Al Albertson.
Description: Minneapolis, MN : Bellwether Media, Inc., [2020] | Series:
   Blastoff! readers: animals of the forest | Includes bibliographical
   references and index. | Audience: Ages 5-8 | Audience: Grades K-1 |
   Summary: "Relevant images match informative text in this introduction to
   gray wolves. Intended for students in kindergarten through third
   grade"-- Provided by publisher.
Identifiers: LCCN 2019024657 (print) | LCCN 2019024658 (ebook) | ISBN
   9781644871263 (library binding) | ISBN 9781618918024 (ebook)
Subjects: LCSH: Gray wolf--Juvenile literature.
Classification: LCC QL737.C22 A38 2020 (print) | LCC QL737.C22 (ebook) | DDC 599.773--dc23
LC record available at https://lccn.loc.gov/2019024657
LC ebook record available at https://lccn.loc.gov/2019024658

Editor: Betsy Rathburn   Designer: Josh Brink

Printed in the United States of America, North Mankato, MN.

Table of Contents

Life in the Forest

Gray wolves are large **mammals**. They make homes all around the world.

They are often found in the forest **biome**.

Gray Wolf Range

N
W E
S

range = ☐

Gray wolves are **adapted** to the forest. Dull colors help them blend in.

guard hairs

Thick fur with stiff **guard hairs** keeps the wolves warm in winter.

Snowy winters make travel tough. Narrow chests help gray wolves cut through deep snow.

Special Adaptations

narrow
chest

thick fur

big paws

Big paws help them
walk on top of snow.

Wolf Packs

pack

Forest life can be hard.
Gray wolves live in
packs to stay safe.

Most packs have around ten wolves. Each pack has a strong leader.

Packs **communicate** over long distances. They **howl** to mark **territories** and find lost pack members.

Their howls carry
for many miles!

Packs travel through
large territories.
They must work hard
to find enough food.

They hunt together to
take down large **prey**!

Gray Wolf Stats

Least Concern	Near Threatened	Vulnerable	Endangered	Critically Endangered	Extinct in the Wild	Extinct

conservation status: least concern

life span: 6 to 8 years

Gray wolves are **carnivores**. Their favorite meals are elk and deer.

Gray wolves can eat up to 20 pounds (9 kilograms) in one meal!

Gray Wolf Diet

deer

sheep

elk

Gray wolves are top forest **predators**. They easily spot movement between trees.

Long legs help them
chase prey for miles.
They can run almost 40 miles
(70 kilometers) per hour!

Gray wolves have strong teeth and jaws. Some of their teeth are over 2 inches (5 centimeters) long!

Gray wolves are the strongest hunters in the forest!

Glossary

adapted—well suited due to changes over a long period of time

biome—a large area with certain plants, animals, and weather

carnivores—animals that only eat meat

communicate—to share information and feelings

guard hairs—long, thick hairs on the outside of a gray wolf's coat

howl—to let out a long, loud cry

mammals—warm-blooded animals that have backbones and feed their young milk

packs—groups of wolves that live and hunt together

predators—animals that hunt other animals for food

prey—animals that are hunted by other animals for food

territories—the land areas where animals live

To Learn More

AT THE LIBRARY

Grack, Rachel. *Wolves*. Mankato, Minn.: Amicus, 2019.

Kenney, Karen Latchana. *Saving the Gray Wolf*. Minneapolis, Minn.: Jump!, 2019.

O'Brien, Cynthia J. *Bringing Back the Gray Wolf*. New York, N.Y.: Crabtree Publishing, 2019.

ON THE WEB

FACTSURFER

Factsurfer.com gives you a safe, fun way to find more information.

1. Go to www.factsurfer.com.

2. Enter "gray wolves" into the search box and click 🔍.

3. Select your book cover to see a list of related web sites.

Index

The images in this book are reproduced through the courtesy of: Don Mammoser, front cover (gray wolf); SOMCHAI BOONPUN, front cover (rocks); Nomad_Soul, front cover (background); Aleksey Stemmer, p. 2-3; Artiste2d3d, p. 3; Jim Cumming, p. 4; Dennis W Donohue, pp. 6, 8; David Osborn, pp. 7, 17 (bottom); Holly Kuchera, pp. 9 (all), 16; Andyworks, p. 10; Frenchwildlifephotograher, p. 11; Nagel Photography, p. 12; Ronnie Howard, p. 13; Lori Ellis, p. 14; blickwinkel/ Alamy, p. 15; Paul Tessier, p. 17 (left); Nataliia Melnychuk, p. 17 (right); Marcia Straub, p. 18; Warren Metcalf, p. 19; Thyrymn2, p. 20; Waitandshoot, p. 21; miroslav chytil, p. 22.